ices

ices

sorbets, granitas, lollies and more

Sunil Vijayakar   **photography by Richard Jung**

RYLAND
PETERS
& SMALL

LONDON NEW YORK

First published in the
United Kingdom in 2007
by Ryland Peters & Small
20–21 Jockey's Fields
London WC1R 4BW
www.rylandpeters.com

10 9 8 7 6 5 4 3 2 1

Printed in China

ISBN: 978-1-84597-384-1

A CIP record for this book is available from
the British Library.

Design and photographic art direction
  Steve Painter
Commissioning Editor Julia Charles
Senior Editors Clare Double,
  Lesley Malkin
Production Simon Walsh
Art Director Anne-Marie Bulat
Publishing Director Alison Starling

Home Economist Sunil Vijayakar
Prop Stylist Roisin Nield

Acknowledgments
With thanks to Magimix
(www.magimix.com) for the loan and
use of their ice-cream maker.

Thanks also to Richard Jung for his
amazing photography and to Mary Wall
for assisting me in testing all the recipes
for the book.

Notes
• All spoon measurements are level unless
otherwise specified.
• All eggs are large unless otherwise
specified. Uncooked or partly cooked eggs
should not be served to the very young,
the very old, those with compromised
immune systems or to pregnant women.

contents

everybody loves an iced treat

It is easy to make your own delicious, colourful and healthy iced treats, experimenting with different combinations of flavours and fruits. Recipes are given for lollies and pops (fruit purées and juices mixed and frozen solid in moulds), sorbets (usually a simple sugar-syrup base flavoured and lightened with egg white), iced soufflés (the basic sorbet mixture but frozen in individual dishes, sometimes with gelatine for a slightly softer texture), frozen yoghurts (yoghurt with fruit, fruit purées or sweeteners and frozen in moulds), granitas (their texture is granular since the mixture is beaten not churned), sherbets (like sorbets, with milk or cream added; these are made with low-fat yoghurt and fat-free fromage frais), water ices (like sorbets but without egg white, making them denser and more intensely flavoured) and finally frappés and slushes (flavoured fruit and sugar mixtures blitzed in the food processor, once frozen, to make them smooth but thick).

Ice-cream makers aren't strictly necessary, but make the job faster and easier, and the texture slightly smoother. One with a built-in freezing unit is best – your ice cream can be ready in less than 30 minutes.

To make ices by hand, called still-freezing, set your freezer at −18°C (0°F). Cover and freeze the mixture in a freezer-proof container for ½–1 hour. Remove and beat with an electric whisk or in a food processor until the ice crystals are smooth, working quickly to minimize melting. Cover and return to the freezer, repeating 2–3 more times at 1½-hour intervals. After the final beating, allow the mixture to freeze for 2–3 hours or overnight before using. Soften very hard ices in the refrigerator for 15–20 minutes before serving.

iced lollies and pops

Cranberry and mango make for a fabulous fruity combination. This recipe couldn't be simpler and the bars look beautiful too.

cranberry and mango bars

300 ml cranberry juice

300 ml fresh mango purée

6 rectangular moulds

makes 6

Half fill your mould with the cranberry juice. Freeze for a few hours until set and top with the mango purée. Freeze again until completely frozen.

Tip: To make really good mango purée, buy the freshest, ripest and sweetest mangoes available, skin and stone them and then blitz in a processor until smooth.

crushed ice sticks (golas)

These are one of the easiest, most delightful iced treats for a hot summer's day. Use whatever fruit syrup or cordial you desire and, for adults only, these 'golas' are great to dip into any liqueur of your choice.

300 g finely crushed ice

any fruit-based syrup or cordial such as strawberry, elderflower, rose, lemon, orange or blackcurrant

6 wooden or bamboo skewers

makes 6

Take about 50 g crushed ice in the palm of your hand and mould it around the end of a wooden or bamboo skewer, pressing tightly so the ice forms into a rough lollipop shape.

Fill small glasses with the syrup of your choice, dip the gola into the syrup and then suck the syrup through the ice. Keep dipping until the ice is gone.

ice-cube treats

Make pretty flavoured decorations for your drinks or a large punch-bowl by adding slices of fruit, berries and herbs to ice-cube containers. Fill with still or sparkling water and freeze until firm.

You can also freeze fruit juices in the ice-cube trays and then add to long glasses of chilled soda or sparkling water.

Suggested ice-cube ingredients

fruit:

star-fruit, sliced

lemons, sliced

oranges, sliced

kiwi fruit, sliced

green, red or black grapes, whole or sliced

berries:

blackberries, whole

raspberries, whole

small strawberries, whole

blueberries, whole

red, black and white currants

herbs:

basil leaves

mint leaves

rosemary sprigs

lemon balm leaves

The combination of strawberries and cream is a guaranteed favourite with everyone. Show them how much you care with this heart-healthy version.

iced strawberry hearts

500 g fresh or good-quality frozen strawberries, hulled and roughly chopped

75 g golden caster sugar

300 ml low-fat vanilla-flavoured yoghurt

6 heart-shaped moulds

makes 6

Place the strawberries and sugar in a food processor and blend until smooth. Fill the heart moulds halfway up with this strawberry purée and freeze for several hours or until set. Top with the vanilla yoghurt and freeze until completely frozen.

Dip the moulds in hot water for a few seconds to unmould and serve immediately.

mint julep sticks

A grown-up icy treat, perfect as a fun aperitif or perhaps a light dessert on a balmy summer's evening. To make a child-friendly version, simply leave out the bourbon.

300 g sugar

50 g fresh mint leaves, finely chopped

15 ml bourbon

mint leaves, to decorate

6 ice lolly moulds and 6 lolly sticks

makes 6

Place the sugar in a saucepan with 600 ml water, heat and stir until the sugar has completely dissolved. Boil for a minute or two, then remove from the heat and add the chopped mint leaves. Leave to cool completely.

When the mixture is cold, strain out the mint and add the bourbon. Pour into moulds and push whole mint leaves into each one. Insert sticks and place in the freezer until frozen. To serve, dip the moulds into hot water for a few seconds and remove carefully.

mini honey kiwi popsicles

Kiwis are simply packed with vitamin C, and this is a really fun way to ensure you get your recommended dose. For even more impact, add a couple of drops of green food colouring.

4 ripe kiwi fruit, peeled

4–5 tablespoons runny honey

6 mini moulds or fairy-cake cases

6 sticks (optional)

makes 6

Purée the kiwi fruit in a food processor or blender and add the honey to taste – depending on the sweetness of the kiwis you may not need to use all of it. Pour into 6 mini moulds or fairy-cake cases, insert sticks if you wish and freeze for 4–6 hours or until completely frozen.

These fabulous-looking cones are bursting at the seams with fruit, which makes them an utterly delicious and stylish way to get your five-a-day.

mixed berry and citrus cones

500 g mixed berries such as strawberries, raspberries, blackberries and blueberries

100 g icing sugar

200 ml freshly squeezed orange juice

1 tablespoon lime juice

1 tablespoon lemon juice

makes 6

Start by making the cones. Cut out six 15 x 30 cm lengths of greaseproof paper. Twist the greaseproof paper to form a cone shape, making sure that no hole is visible at the pointed end, and staple to secure.

Blitz the berries with the icing sugar in a food processor or blender until smooth. If you wish, use a sieve to strain out all of the seeds. Put the orange juice in a small jug with the lime and lemon juices.

Stand the cones upright in two or three glass tumblers to support them. Spoon the berry mixture into the cone bases, then top with the juice and freeze, standing upright, for 4–6 hours or until firm. To serve, invert the cones onto a plate and gently peel off the greaseproof paper.

o-j lollies

Commercially produced ice lollies are often packed full of sugar and unhealthy additives. Give your children these home-made ones and reduce the family's dental bills.

600 ml freshly squeezed
orange juice

6 ice lolly moulds and 6 lolly sticks

makes 6

Pour the orange juice into the ice lolly moulds. Insert the sticks and freeze for 4–6 hours or until completely solid.

When ready to serve, dip the moulds in hot water for a few seconds to loosen the lollies and serve immediately.

raspberry lollies

Your children will delight in these ruby-coloured treats. For a fun stripy effect, alternate the raspberry mixture with orange juice, freezing each layer before adding the next.

750 g fresh or good-quality
frozen raspberries

4 tablespoons runny honey

6 ice lolly moulds and 6 lolly sticks

makes 6

Purée the raspberries in a food processor or blender. Strain through a sieve to remove the seeds, then add the honey. Pour the mixture into the lolly moulds, insert the sticks and freeze for 4–6 hours or until completely solid.

When ready to serve, dip the moulds in hot water for a few seconds to loosen the lollies and serve immediately.

peach and plum popsicles

A wonderful way to capture the warmth of summer with ripe, juicy peaches and plums. Vary these popsicles by using any fresh fruit purée of your choice.

500 ml fresh peach purée

500 ml fresh plum purée

6 popsicle moulds with sticks

makes 6

Carefully spoon a little of the peach purée into the base of 6 popsicle moulds and top with a little of the plum mixture. Continue layering until the moulds are full. Insert the sticks in the centre and freeze for 4–6 hours or until firm. To serve, dip the moulds in hot water for a few seconds and remove the popsicles.

Tip: To make the peach purée, place 600 g of freshly skinned, stoned and chopped peaches into a saucepan with 200 ml water and sugar to taste. Bring to the boil, reduce the heat to low and simmer gently for 4–5 minutes. Remove from the heat and process until smooth in a food processor. Make the plum purée in the same way with halved and stoned plums.

nectarine and almond sorbet

700 g ripe nectarines, peeled, halved and stoned

75 g golden caster sugar

a few drops of almond extract

1 egg white

ice-cream maker (optional)

makes 600 ml, serves 4–6

This fruity ice is bursting with the flavours of a Mediterranean summer – ripe nectarines delicately flavoured with a hint of almonds.

Thinly slice the nectarines and place in a saucepan with the sugar and 300 ml water. Bring to the boil, reduce the heat to low, cover and simmer for 6–8 minutes or until the nectarines are just tender.

Transfer to a food processor or blender and blend until smooth. Allow to cool and then chill.

Add the almond extract, transfer to an ice-cream maker and churn until thick. If making by hand, transfer to a shallow freezer-proof container and freeze for 4 hours or until slushy.

Whisk the egg white until just frothy, add to the ice-cream maker and continue to churn until thick enough to scoop. If making by hand, place the mixture in a processor and whiz until softened. Add the egg white, mix well and freeze for 4–6 hours or until firm. Serve small scoops on chilled plates.

sorbets, frozen yoghurts and iced soufflés

Almost any firm-textured, fruit-based sorbet can be frozen into lolly, popsicle or any other ice moulds to make for a terrific and healthy treat. Here we use plum and tangerine for this delicious sorbet.

tangerine and plum sorbet on a stick

800 g ripe plums, halved, stoned and sliced

75 g golden caster sugar

freshly squeezed juice of 2 sweet tangerines

1 small egg white

ice-cream maker (optional)

6 ice lolly moulds and 6 sticks

makes 6

Place the plums, 200 ml water and the sugar in a saucepan and bring to the boil. Cover, reduce the heat to low and cook for 4–5 minutes or until the sugar has dissolved and the plums are just tender. Transfer the mixture to a food processor and blend with the tangerine juice until smooth. Allow the mixture to cool, place in an ice-cream maker and churn until thick. If making the sorbet by hand, place the mixture in a shallow freezer-proof container and freeze for 4 hours until slushy.

Whisk the egg white until frothy and add to the mixture in the ice-cream maker. Continue to churn until thick enough to scoop. You can now place this mixture in any ice lolly mould of your choice, insert a stick and freeze until firm. If making by hand, mix the egg white into the slushy mixture and pour into moulds, insert a stick and freeze until firm.

To serve, dip the moulds in hot water for 2–3 seconds and remove carefully.

chilli-lime sorbet

A twist on the classic lemon sorbet, this refreshingly tangy, deliciously smooth sorbet has a hidden kick of spiciness from the chilli.

200 g golden caster sugar

1 red chilli, deseeded and very finely chopped

6 large limes

1 egg white

ice-cream maker (optional)

makes about 600 ml, serves 4–6

Place the sugar, 300 ml water and the chilli in a saucepan over a gentle heat and stir occasionally until all the sugar has dissolved. Bring to the boil, remove from the heat and finely grate the zest of 2 of the limes into the mixture. Set aside to cool, then chill.

Squeeze the juice from the limes and add to the syrup. Place the mixture in an ice-cream maker and churn until thick. Alternatively, if making the sorbet by hand, freeze the mixture in a shallow freezer-proof container for 4 hours or until mushy.

Whisk the egg white until just frothy. If using an ice-cream maker, add the whisked egg white and continue to churn until it is thick enough to scoop. If using the hand method, soften the mixture by whizzing it in a food processor, add the whisked egg white and return the sorbet to the tub. Freeze for 4–6 hours or until firm. Serve small scoops of the sorbet in chilled glasses or cups.

blueberry and lemon sorbet

This deliciously sharp sorbet bursts with a wonderful flavour of summer. You can use mixed berries instead of the blueberries.

500 g blueberries

150 g golden caster sugar

finely grated zest and freshly squeezed juice of 1 small lemon

1 egg white

glazed lemon slices and blueberries, to decorate

ice-cream maker (optional)

makes about 600 ml, serves 4–6

Place the blueberries and 150 ml water in a saucepan and bring to the boil. Remove from the heat and purée until smooth. Set aside to cool. Put the sugar, finely grated lemon zest and juice and 200 ml water in a saucepan and heat gently until the sugar has dissolved. Bring to the boil, take off the heat and transfer to a bowl. Cool and chill.

Mix the blueberries and sugar syrup. Transfer to an ice-cream maker and churn until thick or, if making by hand, freeze the mixture in a shallow freezer-proof container for 4 hours or until slushy.

Whisk the egg white until just frothy and follow the instructions given in step 3 of the Chilli-Lime Sorbet recipe (see left). Serve the sorbet in scoops with glazed lemon slices and blueberries to decorate.

120 g golden caster sugar

600 ml champagne

100 ml peach juice

ice-cream maker (optional)

makes about 800 ml, serves 4–6

champagne sorbet

This grown-up sorbet makes a very elegant finale to a sophisticated meal. I have used champagne here but the recipe will work equally well with any sparkling wine, such as Italian prosecco or Spanish cava.

Place the sugar in a saucepan with 120 ml water and heat gently until the sugar has dissolved. Bring to the boil and remove from the heat. Allow to cool.

Add the champagne and peach juice to the sugar syrup and churn in an ice-cream maker until just thick enough to scoop. Alternatively, if making by hand place in a shallow freezer-proof container and freeze for 4–6 hours, whisking the partially frozen mixture at least twice during the process.

Scoop into chilled glasses or bowls and serve immediately.

This wonderfully speckled, pale green sorbet is made using ripe kiwis and is given a lively aromatic flavour by the addition of stem ginger. For a stronger flavour, omit the stem ginger and use a teaspoon of freshly grated ginger instead.

kiwi and stem ginger sorbet

115 g golden caster sugar

8 ripe kiwi fruit, peeled and roughly chopped

1 egg white, lightly beaten

2 tablespoons stem ginger, drained and finely chopped

ice-cream maker (optional)

makes 600 ml, serves 4–6

Place the sugar and 300 ml water in a small saucepan and heat gently until the sugar has dissolved. Bring to the boil and remove from the heat. Allow to cool and then chill.

Place the kiwi fruit in a blender and process until smooth. Add this to the chilled syrup and stir to mix well.

If using an ice-cream maker, churn the mixture until thick, add the egg white and stem ginger and churn until firm enough to scoop. Freeze until ready to serve.

If making the sorbet by hand, pour the mixture into a shallow freezer-proof container, stir in the egg white and allow to freeze for 3–4 hours. Place in a food processor, process until smooth and return to the freezer, repeating this process once more. Stir in the stem ginger and freeze for 3–4 hours until firm.

Natural yoghurt is flavoured with maple syrup and finely chopped fresh peach for these healthy iced treats. Vary the flavour of the yoghurt and use different fruit to make your own versions of these yoghurt squares.

maple-peach frozen yoghurt squares

500 ml natural yoghurt

150 ml maple syrup

250 g fresh peaches, peeled, stoned and finely chopped

ice-cream maker (optional)

6 square moulds and 6 lolly sticks

makes 6

Place the yoghurt in a bowl and stir in the maple syrup. Fold in the peaches and combine well.

Place the mixture in an ice-cream maker and churn until firm enough to scoop. If making by hand, pour the mixture into a shallow freezer-proof container and freeze for 2 hours, whisking the partially frozen ice at least once.

Remove the mixture from the ice-cream maker or container and spoon into individual square moulds (approximately 5 cm square) or any other mould of your choice. Insert the sticks and freeze until firm. To serve, dip the moulds in hot water for 2–3 seconds and carefully remove the squares.

Variation: Substitute 250 g of finely chopped fresh pineapple for the peaches to make Tropical Pineapple Frozen Yoghurt.

Colourful, tasty and healthy, these iced desserts make a great 'snack-attack' standby. Keep a batch of these in the freezer for unexpected young visitors.

marbled strawberry and blackberry yoghurt cups

250 g blackberries

250 g strawberries

8 tablespoons honey

500 g natural yoghurt

6 cup moulds, each about 7 cm in diameter

makes 6

Purée the blackberries and strawberries separately in a food processor until smooth. Using a sieve and spatula, strain the mixtures into separate bowls and add 2 tablespoons of the honey to each one. Stir to mix well.

Mix the yoghurt with the remaining honey.

Spoon some blackberry mixture into the base of a cup mould. Carefully spoon over some yoghurt mixture and then some strawberry mixture. Using a skewer, lightly marble the mixture.

Repeat with the other 5 moulds and freeze for 4–6 hours or until firm. To serve, dip the moulds in hot water for 2–3 seconds, remove and serve immediately.

This is a dramatic and elegant dessert which, unlike its hot relative, will not collapse on serving and can be made well in advance. Be prepared for some serious 'oohs' and 'aahs' from your guests.

mixed berry iced soufflés

350 g mixed berries such as raspberries, strawberries and blackberries

120 g caster sugar

2 egg whites

55 g icing sugar

450 ml fromage frais

6 single-portion ramekins or short paper cups

makes 6

Make 6 strips of double-thickness greaseproof or parchment paper to form collars around the outsides of 6 ramekins, each coming 3 cm above the rim. Wrap and secure each collar with a pin or cocktail stick and chill the ramekins until ready to use.

Set aside 12 of your nicest-looking berries to decorate the soufflés. Purée the remaining berries in a food processor and then press through a sieve to remove the seeds. Stir in the caster sugar and set aside for at least 1 hour to allow the sugar to dissolve and the flavours to develop.

Whisk the egg whites until they form soft peaks, then add the icing sugar and continue to whisk until glossy and firm. Beat the fromage frais lightly just to loosen it.

With a large spoon or spatula gently fold the berry purée, egg whites and fromage frais together. Spoon into the prepared ramekins, smooth the tops and cover with foil, taking care that the foil does not touch the tops of the soufflés. Freeze until firm.

5–10 minutes before serving, remove from the freezer and take off the foil and collars. Place in the refrigerator to soften a little for 5 minutes and then decorate with the reserved berries.

Who doesn't love a creamy dreamy lemon dessert?
This one ticks all the boxes and then some thanks
to the addition of cardamom. And it's low-fat to boot.

spiced citrus frozen soufflés

1 tablespoon powdered gelatine

2 egg whites

200 g icing sugar

finely grated zest and freshly
squeezed juice of 3 lemons

½ teaspoon ground cardamom

450 ml fromage frais

6 single-portion ramekins
or small glasses

makes 6

Make 6 strips of double-thickness greaseproof or parchment paper to form collars around the outsides of 6 ramekins, each coming 3 cm above the rim. Wrap and secure each collar with a pin or cocktail stick and chill the ramekins until ready to use.

Sprinkle the gelatine over 4 tablespoons of cold water in a small pan and set aside for 4 minutes until the gelatine has softened. Heat very gently, stirring, without allowing to boil until the gelatine has completely melted. Set aside.

Whisk the egg whites until they form soft peaks, then add 100 g of the icing sugar and continue to whisk until glossy and firm. Fold in the lemon zest and juice and ground cardamom.

Beat the fromage frais and remaining icing sugar lightly just to loosen, then fold in the softened gelatine.

With a large spoon or spatula gently fold together the fromage frais and egg white mixtures. Spoon into the prepared ramekins, smooth the tops and cover with foil, taking care that the foil does not touch the tops of the soufflés. Freeze until firm.

Remove from the freezer 5–10 minutes before serving and take off the foil and collars. Place in the refrigerator for 5 minutes to soften a little, then serve.

granitas, sherbets and water ices

A perfectly ripe apricot is a rare and wonderful treat, however you enjoy it. This sherbet is no exception.

apricot and grape sherbet

100 g caster sugar

12 ripe apricots, halved and stoned

150 ml grape juice

300 g natural yoghurt or fromage frais

ice-cream maker

makes 600 ml, serves 4–6

Make a syrup by gently heating 150 ml water and the sugar in a pan, stirring to dissolve the sugar. Add the apricots and simmer for 5 minutes. Remove from the heat and leave to cool.

Once cooled, transfer the apricots and syrup to a food processor or blender and process until smooth. Press through a sieve and stir in the grape juice and yoghurt or fromage frais.

Transfer the mixture to an ice-cream maker and churn until thick. Spoon into a plastic container and freeze for 4–5 hours or until firm.

Blood oranges have been cultivated in Sicily since ancient times. An unassuming peel, tinged with purple, conceals a flesh ranging from rose to almost black: pure drama, especially in this festive ice.

blood orange water ice

8 large blood oranges

115 g caster sugar

ice-cream maker

makes about 600 ml, serves 4–6

Wash the oranges in hot water to remove any waxy coating.

Put the sugar and 200 ml water in a saucepan. Using a zester or vegetable peeler, pare thin strips of the zest from 1 of the oranges and add to the sugar and water. Heat gently, stirring until the sugar has completely dissolved. Bring to the boil and then remove from the heat and leave to cool. Strain out the zest, juice the oranges and add the juice to the syrup.

Transfer the mixture to an ice-cream maker and churn until it holds its shape. Spoon into a shallow plastic container and freeze for 3 hours. Remove from the freezer, beat for a minute or two and return to the freezer for a couple of hours or until firm enough to scoop.

Tip: If you are unable to find fresh blood oranges, use 600 ml of a good shop-bought blood-orange juice instead.

espresso granita

A refreshing 'pick-me-up', great after a lazy summer lunch. The cardamom lends it an exotic hint of mystery. If you have nothing planned for the afternoon, try adding a tablespoon or two of coffee liqueur.

5 tablespoons good-quality
espresso or strong filter coffee

1 litre boiling water

150 g caster sugar

¼ teaspoon ground cardamom

2 tablespoons Kahlúa or other
coffee liqueur (optional)

makes about 600 ml, serves 4–6

Prepare your coffee in a cafetière or filter machine. If using a cafetière, leave to stand for 5 minutes after adding the water before plunging. Pour the coffee into a large shallow plastic container and add the sugar. Stir until completely dissolved, then add the cardamom and Kahlúa, if using, and leave the mixture to cool.

Cover and freeze for 2 hours or until the coffee mixture is starting to look mushy.

Break up the ice crystals with a fork and finely mash them. Return the granita to the freezer for another 2 hours, mashing every 30 minutes until the ice forms fine, even crystals. After the final mashing return to the freezer for at least an hour before serving.

green tea and mint granita

A sophisticated and refreshing take on iced tea – just looking at the minty green colour will make you feel cooler!

150 g caster sugar

3 green tea teabags

30 g fresh mint leaves

makes about 600 ml, serves 4–6

Place the sugar and 600 ml water in a saucepan, heat gently and stir until dissolved. Bring to the boil and remove from the heat. Add the teabags and leave to infuse for 5 minutes. Meanwhile, finely chop the mint leaves.

Remove the teabags from the pan and allow the syrup to cool completely. When it is cool, add the finely chopped mint leaves and stir through.

Pour the mixture into a large, shallow plastic container and freeze for 2 hours. Remove from the freezer and with a fork mash up any crystals that have formed. Return to the freezer for another 2 hours and repeat the mashing. Freeze for at least another hour before serving.

pomegranate granita

This once hard-to-find fruit, a native of the Middle East, has a thick waxy skin enclosing hundreds of jewel-like ruby seeds. The juice is hailed as a great antioxidant and is now widely available in many shops.

200 g caster sugar

600 ml pomegranate juice

pomegranate seeds,
to decorate (optional)

makes about 600 ml, serves 4–6

In a large shallow plastic container, stir the sugar into the juice until dissolved.

Cover and freeze for 2 hours or until the mixture is starting to look mushy.

Using a fork, break up the ice crystals and finely mash them. Return the granita to the freezer for another 2 hours, mashing every 30 minutes, until the ice forms fine, even crystals. After the final mashing return to the freezer for at least an hour before serving. Decorate with the fresh pomegranate seeds, if using.

orange and lemon granita

Zing zing zing! Your taste buds won't know what's hit them. Zesty doesn't even begin to describe this wide-awake, citrus assault on the senses.

115 g caster sugar

6 oranges

2 lemons

makes about 600 ml, serves 4–6

Put the sugar and 200 ml water into a saucepan. Using a zester or vegetable peeler, pare thin strips of zest from 1 orange and 1 lemon and add them to the sugar and water. Heat gently, stirring until the sugar has completely dissolved. Bring to the boil and then remove from the heat and leave to cool. When cold, strain the liquid into a large shallow plastic container.

Juice the fruit and stir into the syrup to combine. Freeze for 2 hours. Remove from the freezer and with a fork mash up any crystals that have formed. Return to the freezer for another 2 hours and repeat the mashing process. Freeze again for at least 1 more hour before serving.

spicy plum sherbet

Curl up and take comfort from summer's parting gift. This cold-yet-warming spicy plum sherbet is perfect for those early autumn days when plums still abound yet there is a decided nip in the air.

120 g caster sugar

1 cinnamon stick

4 cloves

2.5 cm fresh ginger, peeled and sliced

12 ripe plums, halved and stoned

375 g low-fat natural yoghurt

ice-cream maker

makes about 600 ml, serves 4–6

Put the sugar, cinnamon, cloves, ginger and 100 ml water in a saucepan and heat gently, stirring to dissolve the sugar. Add the plums and simmer for 5 minutes. Remove from the heat and leave to cool.

Once cool, discard the cinnamon and cloves, transfer the plums and syrup to a food processor or blender and process until smooth. Press through a sieve into a bowl and stir in the yoghurt.

Transfer the mixture to an ice-cream maker and churn until thick. Spoon into a plastic container and freeze for 4–5 hours or until firm.

raspberry sherbet

Pink, creamy and luscious – this sherbet sounds far naughtier than it actually is! Fresh berries and fat-free fromage frais make for a delightfully low-fat treat.

120 g caster sugar

375 g raspberries

375 g fat-free fromage frais

ice-cream maker

makes about 600 ml, serves 4–6

Gently heat the sugar and 100 ml water in a saucepan, stirring to dissolve the sugar. Bring to the boil and remove from the heat.

Purée the raspberries in a food processor or blender. Press through a sieve to remove the seeds. Stir into the cold syrup and chill until very cold.

Add the fromage frais to the purée and whisk until smooth.

Transfer the mixture to an ice-cream maker and churn until thick. Spoon into a plastic container and freeze for 4–5 hours or until firm.

This would be the perfect ending to an Eastern-inspired meal. Star anise and mandarin oranges are natural partners as both originate in China. The star anise not only adds a wonderful liquorice flavour, it also looks stunning and makes for a very stylish decoration.

star anise and mandarin orange granita

150 g sugar

6 whole star anise

20 mandarin oranges

makes about 600 ml, serves 4–6

Put the sugar and 200 ml water in a saucepan and heat gently, stirring until the sugar has completely dissolved. Add the star anise and simmer without stirring for 2 minutes. Remove from the heat and leave to cool.

Cut a slice off the top and bottom of each mandarin, then slice away the peel and pith. Chop the flesh roughly and process in a food processor until almost smooth. Press the resulting pulp through a sieve into a large shallow plastic container. Strain the syrup into the same container, reserving the star anise. Mix well, cover and freeze for 2 hours or until the mixture is starting to look mushy.

Using a fork, break up and finely mash the ice crystals. Return the granita to the freezer for another 2 hours, mashing every 30 minutes, until the ice forms fine, even crystals. After the final mashing return to the freezer for at least an hour before serving. Decorate with the reserved star anise if you wish.

On a sticky summer day there is nothing better than sinking your teeth into a slice of refrigerator-cold watermelon. Nothing, that is, except this vivid granita with a hint of lime.

watermelon granita

150 g caster sugar

1.75 kg watermelon

finely grated zest and freshly squeezed juice of 1 lime

makes about 600 ml, serves 4–6

Put the sugar and 150 ml water in a pan and slowly bring to the boil, stirring to dissolve the sugar. Once boiled, remove from the heat and leave to cool.

Scoop out the flesh from the watermelon and discard the seeds. Blitz briefly in a food processor until smooth and then strain through a sieve into a large shallow plastic container. Add the syrup, lime zest and lime juice and mix well.

Freeze for 2 hours. Remove from the freezer and with a fork mash any crystals that have formed. Return to the freezer for another 2 hours and repeat the mashing process. Freeze for at least 1 more hour before serving.

frappés, slushes and frozen drinks

This tropical, thick and cooling sorbet-drink evokes memories of golden beaches, azure seas and swaying palm trees. For a child-friendly version, omit the rum.

iced piña colada

300 g ripe fresh pineapple, chopped

75 g sugar

200 ml coconut milk

4 tablespoons white rum

ice-cream maker

makes about 500 ml, serves 2

Stir the pineapple with the sugar to mix well. Leave to stand for 10 minutes at room temperature to allow the sugar to dissolve into the chopped pineapple. Place all the ingredients in an ice-cream maker and churn until softly slushy. Pour into chilled glasses and serve immediately.

frozen strawberry fruit soda

Scoops of sorbet, served in a froth of sparkling zesty soda, would make a perfect treat for many children. This refreshing soda has great adult appeal too.

Strawberry sorbet

500 g strawberries, roughly chopped

150 golden caster sugar

freshly squeezed juice of 1 lime

ice-cream maker

To serve

100 g raspberries

200 ml chilled sparkling organic lemonade (or other soda of your choice)

makes about 600 ml, serves 2

Make the sorbet by placing all the ingredients in a saucepan with 300 ml water and bringing to the boil. Reduce the heat to low and gently simmer for 3–4 minutes. Remove from the heat and when cool process in a blender until smooth. Churn the mixture in an ice-cream maker until thick and then transfer to a shallow freezer-proof container or ice-cube trays and freeze until firm.

Place 2 tall glasses in the freezer to chill for 10 minutes. Place 3 scoops or cubes of the sorbet into the base of each glass. Add the raspberries and top up each glass with the sparkling lemonade.

frozen apple and cinnamon spritzer

The fresh flavours of apple juice infused with cinnamon make a lovely icy drink with a fizzy topping of sparkling wine. For children, replace the sparkling wine with ginger ale.

300 ml clear apple juice

2 cinnamon sticks

about 100 ml chilled sparkling white wine

makes about 300 ml, serves 2

Place the apple juice and cinnamon in a small saucepan and bring to the boil. Remove from the heat and allow to cool. Discard the cinnamon sticks. Transfer to a shallow freezer-proof container and freeze for about 2 hours or until a layer of ice crystals has formed around the edges. Mash with a fork and return to the freezer for another 2–3 hours or until almost solid.

Spoon the apple ice into a food processor and briefly process until very slightly slushy. Transfer to 2 chilled glasses and top with the chilled sparkling wine.

Here pears are combined with rich-flavoured plums to make a smooth and beautifully coloured slush with a gentle hint of rosemary. Choose sweet pears and plums and always use the ripest fruit for natural sweetness.

pear and plum slush

1 pear (approximately 200 g)

400 g plums, halved and stoned

150 g caster sugar

1 small sprig of rosemary

ice-cream maker (optional)

makes about 600 ml, serves 4–6

Peel, core and roughly chop the pear. Put in a saucepan with the plums, sugar, rosemary and 450 ml water. Place over a gentle heat and bring to the boil. Reduce the heat to low and cook gently for 10–12 minutes. Discard the rosemary and transfer the mixture to a blender. Process until smooth and sieve.

Churn the mixture in an ice-cream maker until just soft and slushy. If making the slush by hand, place the mixture in a shallow freezer-proof container and freeze for 6–8 hours or until firm. Remove, transfer to a food processor and process until softly slushy. Serve in chilled glasses.

pink grapefruit and basil frappé

Frappés fall somewhere between granitas and slushes and can be eaten with a spoon or sucked with a thick straw (watch out for brain freeze!). Refreshing and not too sweet, this is a delicate pale pink colour flecked with basil and flavoured with its subtle aniseed tones.

220 g caster sugar

4 large pink grapefruit

50 g basil leaves, finely sliced

makes about 600 ml, serves 4–6

Put the sugar and 300 ml water in a pan with the zest of 1 grapefruit. Heat gently, stirring to dissolve the sugar. Simmer for 5 minutes. Leave to cool.

Juice all the grapefruit. Strain the cooled syrup and add the juice and the basil.

Stir well and freeze for 3 hours in a large shallow container or ice-cube trays.

Before serving, transfer to a blender and crush until smooth.

rhubarb and ginger frappé

The ginger and rhubarb weave magic together in this bittersweet, spicy frappé, which is sure to delight all rhubarb lovers.

750 g rhubarb, chopped

100 g caster sugar

2 cm fresh ginger, peeled and finely grated

makes about 600 ml, serves 4–6

Put the rhubarb in a pan with the sugar, ginger and 100 ml water. Cover and cook over a medium heat for 4–5 minutes. Remove from the heat and leave to cool.

Once cold, transfer to a food processor or blender and purée. Freeze for 3 hours in a large shallow container or ice-cube trays.

Before serving, transfer to a blender and crush until smooth.

index